PHOTOGRAPHS BY *BARBARA KARANT*   TEXT ADAPTED BY *TERRY ANN R. NEFF*

DESIGNED BY *STUDIO BLUE*

WITHIN THE *FAIRY CASTLE*

COLLEEN MOORE'S DOLL HOUSE AT
THE MUSEUM OF SCIENCE AND INDUSTRY, CHICAGO

THE MUSEUM OF SCIENCE AND INDUSTRY

CHICAGO

A BULFINCH PRESS BOOK   LITTLE, BROWN AND COMPANY

BOSTON   NEW YORK   TORONTO   LONDON

THE MUSEUM OF SCIENCE AND
INDUSTRY, CHICAGO

President and CEO:
Dr. James S. Kahn
Director of Business Administration:
Nancy L. Wright
Manager of Product Development:
Jennifer Wood
Curator: Michael T. Sarna
Exhibit Preparator: John Boca

Designed and produced by
studio blue, Chicago

Text adapted and edited by
Terry Ann R. Neff,
t.a.neff associates, inc.,
Tucson, Arizona

Photography by Barbara Karant,
Karant + Associates, Inc., Chicago,
with the assistance of
Erika Dufour, Darris Harris,
David Seide, and Kurt Witcher

First Edition
ISBN 0-8212-2519-7

Library of Congress
Catalog Number
97-75121

Bulfinch Press is an imprint and
trademark of Little, Brown and
Company, (Inc.)

Published simultaneously in
Canada by Little, Brown &
Company (Canada) Limited

PRINTED IN SINGAPORE

TABLE OF CONTENTS

10' - 3"

CHAPEL
page 37

SMALL HALL
page 35

ALTAR

SACRISTY

LIBRARY
page 25

GREAT HALL
page 47

MAGIC
page

DRAWING ROOM
page 59

page 67

DINING ROOM

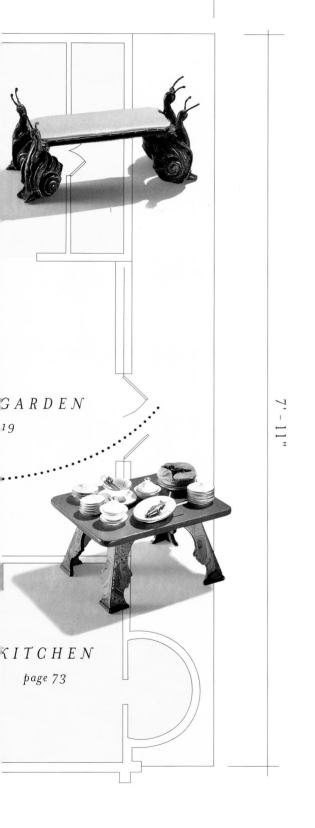

GARDEN
19

KITCHEN
page 73

7' - 11"

RESIDENCE FOR
FAIRY PRINCE AND PRINCESS

CHICAGO   ILLINOIS

FIRST FLOOR
PLAN

SCALE: 1" = 1' - 0"

DRAWING: 258-A

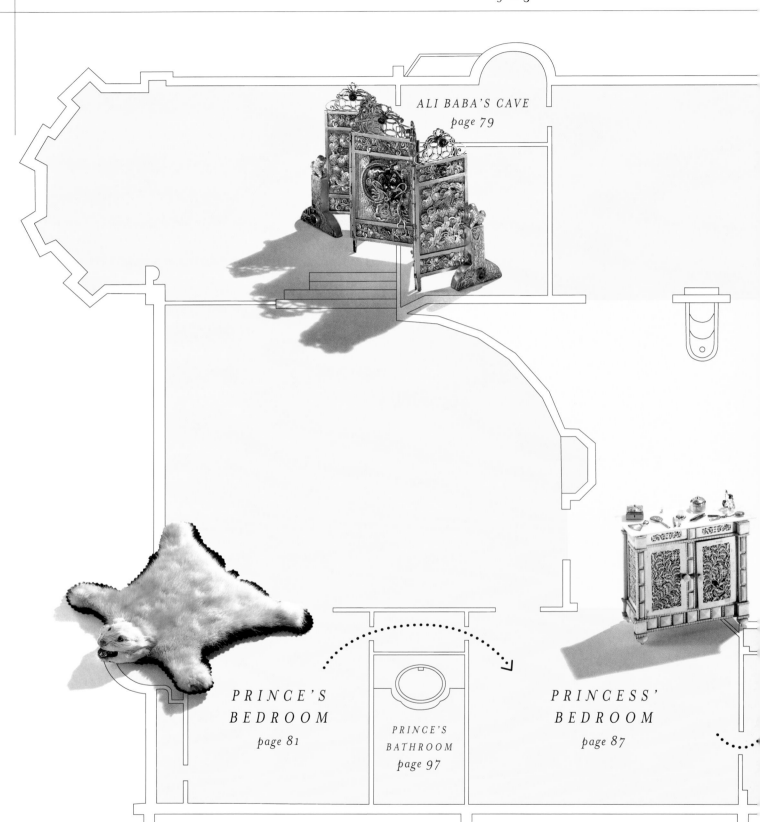

9' - 3"

ALI BABA'S CAVE
page 79

*PRINCE'S
BEDROOM*
page 81

*PRINCE'S
BATHROOM*
page 97

*PRINCESS'
BEDROOM*
page 87

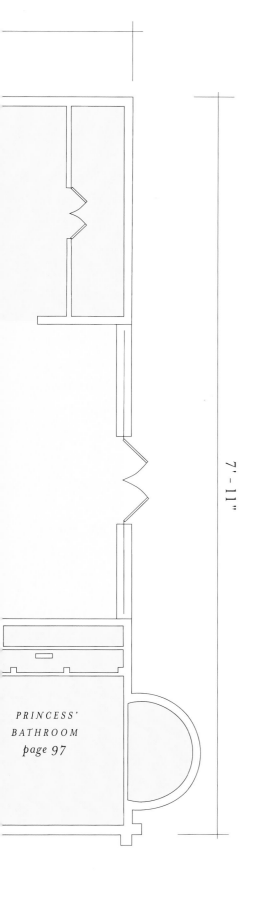

7' - 11"

PRINCESS'
BATHROOM
page 97

page 97

RESIDENCE FOR
FAIRY PRINCE AND PRINCESS

CHICAGO   ILLINOIS

| SECOND AND THIRD FLOOR PLANS | SCALE: 1" = 1' - 0" |
| | DRAWING: 258-B |

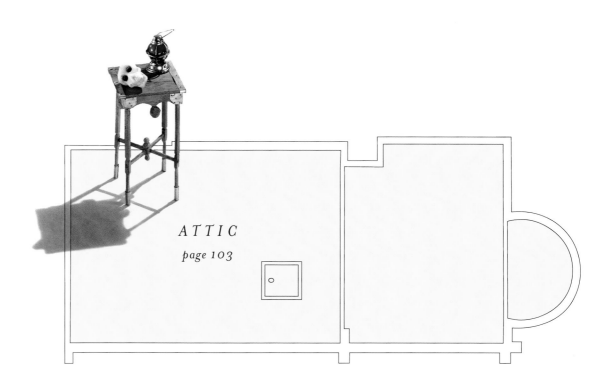

ATTIC
page 103

page 103

FOREWORD AND ACKNOWLEDGMENTS

THE LATE COLLEEN MOORE LEFT BEHIND many legacies: as an actress she was one of the most popular stars of the silent-film era. As a business woman, she skillfully negotiated her contracts and subsequently wrote a book about how to succeed in the stock market. But what she is most cherished for by millions of visitors here at The Museum of Science and Industry is the Fairy Castle.

The castle was built during the Great Depression, when Colleen Moore was recovering from a failed first marriage. It debuted at Macy's in New York and then traveled throughout the United States raising over a half-million dollars for children's charities before coming to rest in Chicago. The perfectly scaled, fanciful rooms were created by Hollywood set designers and embody the work of over 700 artisans who gave form to the fairy tales and fantasies that provide the themes for the castle.

It is with great pleasure that we make *Within the Fairy Castle* available to the public. We hope that the magic of these photographs and the warmth of Colleen Moore's story will inspire other imaginations to take flight.

MICHAEL T. SARNA, CURATOR

THE COLLECTIONS DEPARTMENT OF THE Museum of Science and Industry, and the entire museum staff, especially John Boca, have been invaluable in their ongoing efforts to ensure that the castle is perfectly maintained and accessible to the visiting public. We would like especially to thank the museum's product development team for their management and studio blue for their design of this publication, which will enable audiences all over the world to enjoy the castle — even "after hours." Barbara Karant and Karant + Associates, Inc. have done a superb job in photographing the tiny, precious objects and the intricate, elaborate spaces of the castle. Terry Ann R. Neff of t.a. neff associates, inc., skillfully adapted the text from the original manuscript by Colleen Moore and additional material by Scott H. Rose.

Above all, The Museum of Science and Industry gratefully acknowledges the late Colleen Moore and her family for the donation of the Fairy Castle, their continued support, and the opportunity to bring joy to millions of visitors through the timeless magic of illusion.

DR. JAMES S. KAHN, PRESIDENT AND CEO

THE

FAIRY

CASTLE

A BRIEF

HISTORY

C

olleen Moore often described her castle, a gift to the children of the world, as a doll house, yet she never placed any dolls inside. She intended the castle to be a home for the fantasy characters that had delighted her as a child. And just as she herself was free to imagine its residents, she wanted viewers to have the same opportunity to people it with the fairy-tale characters of their own imaginations and renew the fantasy afresh each time. FOLLOWING THE SAME MIGRATION AS Moore herself, the castle was "created" in Los Angeles and ended up in Chicago, where it is now on permanent display in the Museum of Science and Industry. The nine-foot-square building was designed and constructed in Hollywood on a scale of one inch to the foot. The tallest tower stands seven feet high and the entire structure, although made of aluminum, weighs approximately one ton. Professionals were responsible for the castle: Horace Jackson, a California architect who specialized in set design for First National Studios, drew the plans; the interiors were created by Harold Grieve, who also redesigned Moore's Hollywood mansion; Moore's personal cameraman, Henry Freulich, planned the lighting, which was installed by a master electrician, who also acted as construction foreman.

LEFT: Colleen Moore in her "doll house."

The details are remarkably comprehensive: the elaborate lighting system had to be devised to accommodate bulbs the size of a grain of wheat. A waterworks concealed in one of the towers supplies running water to all the minute spigots; distilled water, used to prevent corrosion of the tiny pipes, is recirculated through the plumbing by a centrifugal pump. Moore's father served as chief engineer and was in charge of the project, which took seven years to complete. From 1928 to 1935, more than a hundred people worked on the castle, including a number of miniature experts from First National who were trained in the production of simulated natural disasters and catastrophes too costly to film in full scale.

Built to be taken apart, packed, and shipped, the castle separates into 200 interlocking pieces. Each room is a separate unit, with lighting and plumbing that can be disconnected or reconnected in one operation. The rooms were constructed first in wood, then cast in aluminum, and finally polished by a jeweler and prepared for decoration. Only then were they assembled according to the blueprints.

Perhaps only in 1920s Hollywood could such a fantasy have been achieved. It was a time of splendid extravagance and carefree self-indulgence: the castle cost almost $500,000 in the hard currency of the 1920s, and it could not be reproduced today at any price; it contains over 2,000 miniature objects from all over the world, many of them unique.

The times were marked as well by a spirit of creativity: the Hollywood studios were filled with artists and craftsmen who welcomed any challenge and took pleasure in the creation of make-believe. Horace Jackson did not look upon the task of designing the castle as a form of humoring Moore. He brought to it not only his architectural skills, but an inspirational concept: "The architecture must have no sense of reality. We must invent a structure that is everybody's conception of an enchanted castle." Harold Grieve was similarly bewitched.

Colleen Moore's own yellow onyx bathroom was the height of luxury.
She could do no less for the Fairy Castle.

"The leading characters of Fairyland will live in this house," Grieve said, as if discussing one of his wealthy clients, "and they will naturally be interested in antiques. They'll want to shop all the auction galleries and antique places in Fairyland, hunting for King Arthur's Round Table to go in the dining room, and Sleeping Beauty's bed. There will have to be a mixture of periods and places. For instance, Aladdin's Lamp will have an oriental connotation. How will that go with pre-Tudor English? We'll have to come up with a new theory of interior design."

Commercial institutions were similarly infected. When Moore contacted a light company that manufactured globes for surgical instruments, they took her seriously at once and developed and produced the grain-of wheat bulbs, which screw into miniscule sockets and sometimes last an entire year. Oriental experts in New York found craftsmen in Beijing to realize the quartz and jade floor Moore desired for the Drawing Room. The chandelier for that room presented a problem, since Moore determined that it should be made of gold and hung with diamonds and emeralds taken from her own jewelry. H. B. Crouch, a prominent and dignified Beverly Hills jeweler, felt that "it would be sacrilege" to use the six-carat diamond pendant along with the diamond necklace and brooch and the emerald bracelet Moore proposed he work with. "Take this home. You have to have something to wear," he insisted. Two weeks later he demanded the return of the pendant, claiming that he needed the diamond for the drop at the bottom of the chandelier. Moore always found it amusing that the elegant Mr. Crouch had succumbed to the charm of the project.

In the years that followed, numerous individuals, many unknown to Moore, proffered their objects or their skills, refusing payment and wishing to remain anonymous. For Moore, the objects evoked the faces of her father and mother, her brother, Cleeve, grandmothers, aunts, uncles, and cousins, friends and colleagues, but also the rapt faces of strangers. Almost every piece has its own story.

THE MAGIC GARDEN

3'- 6" x 4'

We each have our own magic garden. — COLLEEN MOORE

The Fairy Castle is situated in a Magic Garden, a retreat from the mundane realities of everyday living. This area of the Fairy Castle is animated by the endless rocking of the cradle of Rockabye Baby, which, unlike in the lullabye, rests safely and securely in a tiny treetop on a bough that never breaks. BY THE BRONZE POOL IN THE CENTER of the garden stands the Weeping Willow Tree, on which luckless maidens are presumed to have hung their hearts. The willow — perhaps the only one in the world that actually weeps — is in reality a fountain: all its branches are piped with water, so that it showers softly into the pool. The fountain itself tumbles down the stairway banked with flowers. It is a memento of Rome's Spanish Steps at Easter — one of Moore's favorite places. IN THE MIXTURE OF FANTASY AND historical model that alternates throughout the Fairy Castle, the carriage that waits in the garden is a replica of Napoleon's coach, given to Moore by the Fisher brothers of Detroit, designers of automobiles in the early and mid-twentieth century.

BENEATH THE PORCH LIES THE solid-gold, inscribed cornerstone of the castle, laid on April 5, 1935 by Sara Delano Roosevelt, the mother of President Franklin D. Roosevelt, at a gala opening in New York during the castle's tour on behalf of children's charities (above left). In a return to the world of make-believe, the Kitchen wall of the garden displays in bas-relief the story of the Wizard of Oz: Dorothy, the Tin Woodsman, the Straw Man, and the Cowardly Lion are all there, poised to set off on the yellow-brick road to see the "Wonderful Wizard" (above right). The bronze horses that draw the fairy coach were modeled from a painting of the horses that drew the carriage of Queen Elizabeth II to her coronation (left).

A MURAL OF RIP VAN WINKLE SUR–
mounts the door to the Library, and on
the arches are depicted several of Ae–
sop's Fables, including Moore's favor–
ite, "The Fox and the Grapes." Three
plaques on the castle wall represent the
elements: Wind and Rain, the Moon and
Stars, and the glorious Sun.

THIS OBJECT WAS MOORE'S MOST BELOVED in the garden: her Irish grandmother had the golden cradle set with pearls made from a necklace, a pair of earrings, and a brooch she had inherited and worn from child- hood. "It'll be my tombstone," she proph- esied. "More will visit it than my grave." Today more than a million people annu- ally view the Fairy Castle in the Museum of Science and Industry.

THE LIBRARY

2'-3" x 3'-3"

olleen Moore always preferred to "enter" the Fairy Castle through the Library, which opens on to the Magic Garden, rather than through the formal Great Hall. The Library strikes an immediate mood of undersea fantasy: the walls, painted to resemble the ocean, blend into sky near the ceiling. Cold, northern bleakness at one end of the room, epitomized in the depiction of the aurora borealis, gives way at the other end to warm tropical blue and a radiant rainbow marked by a pot of gold at each end. A 500-year-old sandalwood Hindu Buddha is stationed directly under the rainbow's arc. Floor and ceiling work in tandem to capture the heavens, both real and fancied: depicted on the dome are the constellations, while their counterparts, the signs of the zodiac, embellish the floor. THE VERDIGRIS COPPER BOOKSHELVES, lined with tiny books, are the real treasure of the Library. The original collection consisted of sixty-five miniature books on religious subjects, printed in the eighteenth century. These English and French volumes, exquisitely bound in leather, vellum, and gilt, are clearly legible. Among them is perhaps the smallest Bible in the world, printed in 1840, and presented to Moore in 1927 by Antonio Moreno, a famous Hollywood heartthrob and one of her leading men.

Because such books are hard to find, Moore decided to commission modern editions for the Library. She had made a series of one-inch-square books, leather-bound, stamped in gold, with ridged spines. She asked famous writers of her day to put down on their blank pages whatever they chose, in their own handwriting. Edward Albee, Edgar Rice Burroughs, Willa Cather, Noel Coward, Arthur Conan Doyle, Daphne du Maurier, Edna Ferber, F. Scott Fitzgerald, Elinor Glyn, William Randolph Hearst, Aldous Huxley, Sinclair Lewis, Anita Loos, Clare Booth Luce, Adela Rogers St. Johns, John Steinbeck, and Thornton Wilder were among those who contributed.

To the end of her life, Moore kept a half-dozen little blank books, hoping to corner unsuspecting authors. She always felt that perhaps the motto of this sea-struck Library should be Emily Dickinson's line from an untitled poem written around 1873: "There is no frigate like a book to take us lands away."

The most valuable book in the the Library, the autograph album (see page 29), is the only book not on permanent display. It is so valuable that except for special occasions, it is kept in a safe at the Museum of Science and Industry. The album contains the signatures of six American Presidents: Herbert Hoover, Franklin Delano Roosevelt, Harry S. Truman, Dwight D. Eisenhower, Lyndon B. Johnson, and Richard M. Nixon. (Moore deeply regretted that she never acquired the signature of John F. Kennedy; she thought she had plenty of time because he was so young.) Numerous other heads of state and government are represented: Queen Elizabeth II, Prince Philip, the Duke and Duchess of Windsor, Winston Churchill, Charles De Gaulle, Lord Halifax, and Jawaharlal Nehru. The military is represented by General John J. Pershing, General Douglas MacArthur, and Admiral Chester Nimitz. Arturo Toscanini, Pablo Picasso, and Frank Lloyd Wright represent the arts. Orville Wright, Admiral Richard Byrd, John Glenn, Henry Ford, Albert Einstein, and J. P. Morgan are present. Eleanor Roosevelt and Madame Chiang

Kai-shek are among the prominent political women signers. There are many more, and each one has a story all its own. Winston Churchill was at work painting a scene out of the window of his room at the Waldorf Towers in New York when Moore approached him. He stopped just long enough to sign his name. Queen Elizabeth and Prince Philip signed the album at the conclusion of a visit to the Museum of Science and Industry. Indian Prime Minister Jawaharlal Nehru also signed the book following a tour of the castle in the museum. He knew all the fairy tales depicted and was delighted to recognize the characters.

In 1937, when Moore was touring with the Fairy Castle in Detroit, she received a telephone call from Mrs. Henry Ford, who wanted to come see the doll house. Moore invited her to come and bring along her young grandchildren. "It isn't the grandchildren," Mrs. Ford replied. "It's Henry. *He* wants to come." So Henry Ford spent two hours looking at everything in the house with intense interest. With great enthusiasm he signed Moore's autograph album, the first signature in her book.

Moore obtained the signature of Lord Halifax, British Foreign Secretary, in 1938 while crossing the English channel from Paris to London. When she approached her fellow passenger, Lord Halifax gave her a melancholy smile and asked her to hold the book as his left hand was paralyzed. He wrote his name and commented warily, "Tomorrow this may be a very bad name for your book." He and Prime Minister Neville Chamberlain had just signed the Munich Pact with Hitler, allowing him virtually a free hand in Czechoslovakia.

One summer in Cannes, Moore was bemoaning to her husband her numerous failures to obtain Pablo Picasso's signature. The chauffeur overheard and claimed that his girlfriend was Picasso's housekeeper in Cannes, and he could get the autograph. He promised that after the bullfights, his favorite dinner, and a wonderful wine, Picasso would sign the book. Moore was never certain of how it happened, but she got the artist's signature.

BOOK SIGNED
BY EDWARD ALBEE
1 ⅛" x 1"

SEAL WITH GLOBE
4 ½" x 2 ¼" x 2 ¼"

BOOK SIGNED
BY EDNA FERBER
1" x 1"

SHELL CHAIR
2 ½" x 2 ½" x 2"

BOOK SIGNED
BY AGATHA CHRISTIE
1 ⅛" x ¾"

SNAIL BENCH
2 ½" x 5 ½" x 2 ½"

T HE OCEANIC THEME IS CONTIN-
ued throughout the Library. Arches
leading to the Magic Garden are
decorated with seafaring heroes: Gulliver
pulling Lilliputian boats in to shore,
Robinson Crusoe with Friday at his feet.
The fireplace, designed as a massive
fishnet, boasts a painted bronze Neptune
entangled in its folds. On the mantel
Captain Kidd directs the burial of his pirate
treasure. The sea motif extends to the furniture, whose strange, naturalistic shapes
evoke the female water sprite Undine's
underwater palace. The sofas and chaise
longue, with their verdigris copper sea-
shells, sea horses, and sea snails, look as
if they were age-old appurtenances of
nymphs or mermaids.

DICTIONARY ON STAND
5" x 2" x 2"

GAME TABLE
2 ¼" x 1 ¾" x 1 ¾"

CHINESE FIGURINE
3 ¼" x 1 ½" x 1 ½"

My father... gave me my first treasure... when I was five years old... a tiny locket [with] an infinitesimal
dictionary, with all the letters from A to Z printed inside. He explained to me that... I would find inside this book
all the words I ever needed to make life interesting.... — COLLEEN MOORE

THE SMALL HALL

6" x 1'- 6"

IN THE SMALL HALL, A PASSAGEWAY THAT connects the Library and the Chapel, a mural depicts the story of Noah after he has finally brought the ark to land on Mount Ararat. Forty days and forty nights of rain, animals, and family members have taken their toll on Noah, who in this mischievous mural is relaxing from his labors and organizing a small celebration. This earthy reminder was chosen to balance the spirit of the Chapel and the intellect of the Library.

THE CHAPEL

2'- 6" x 4'

In 1926 Moore went to Dublin on a hurried trip expressly to see the Book of Kells, the magnificent late eighth-century illuminated manuscript that is one of Ireland's greatest treasures and was described to Moore as a child by her grandmother. In the Chapel numerous motifs and designs from the book have been reproduced on the ceilings in velvet purples, soft greens, reds, blues, and gold. Scotland is represented as well, in a replica of the Stone of Scone under the seat of the silver throne, a minute copy of the throne in Westminster Abbey where British monarchs sit when they have been crowned. The stone was the ancient rock upon which all kings of Scotland were crowned; the English brought the stone back to London after defeating the Scots centuries ago. THE FLOOR OF THE CHAPEL IS IVORY, designed and carved by Bayard de Volo after a mosaic floor for an Italian palazzo. The central circle depicts God's light, flooding the world. The designs have biblical connotations: sheafs of wheat signifying the years of plenty, the locusts, the Ram, the Dove of Peace, and the Lamb of God.

The stained-glass windows, designed by Helga Brabon, are devoted to Bible stories beloved by children: David and Goliath, Moses in the Bulrushes, the Judgment of Solomon, and Daniel in the Lions' Den. A statue of St. Giles, the beggar saint, guards the Chapel door.

Behind the gold altar, carved as a monument to children, is a tiny copy of Correggio's *Holy Family*. Hanging over the pulpit is a Russian icon set with emeralds and diamonds that was made from a brooch Moore found in an antique shop. Its date is unknown, though it certainly was made long before the Russian Revolution of 1917. The seal originated in the Vatican and was among the treasures lost during the insurrection in the Papal Palace in 1870 when Pius IX was Pope. Moore acquired it at an auction in Boston. The tiny Bible on the prie-dieu was made by David Bryce in Scotland in 1890. The Victorians had a passion for minutiae, and Bryce revived the printing of tiny books, mostly series, on religious subjects. A large collection of Bryce's books are housed in the Library.

The music that pours through the minute gold pipes of the organ is transcribed and played electrically by remote control. Piled on the console are additional musical manuscripts handwritten by composers: Stravinsky's "Firebird Suite," Rachmaninoff's "Prelude," George Gershwin's "Rhapsody in Blue," and two old favorites of Moore's, "The End of a Perfect Day" by Carrie Jacobs Bond and "The Land of the Sky Blue Water" by Charles Wakefield Cadman. Near the organ is an Italian primitive of the Holy Family, and to the right of the organ is a vigil light made of gold and

*…perhaps man has always approached God in the spirit
of a child.* — COLLEEN MOORE

set with diamonds, sapphires, and ru-bies. The large diamond in the sunburst at the top was in Moore's mother's en-gagement ring; she left it to Moore with instructions to use it in the castle. Moore's parents also contributed the small ivory-and-glass vial in the fore-ground, a present to their daughter from their first trip to Italy. The vial contains a cruci-fix that is more than 300 years old and so exquis-itely carved that the head of Christ, which is no larger than the head of a pin, bears an expression of infinite sadness.

Of greatest meaning to Moore in the Chapel was a sliver of wood framed in a gold monstrance designed by David Webb, a gift from Clare Booth Luce, playwright, congresswoman, ambas-sador to Rome, and wife of Henry Luce, founder of *Time* magazine. On a visit to Chicago to see the castle, Luce turned to Moore with tears in her eyes and said she was going to give Moore some-thing for the Chapel in memory of her daughter, who had been killed in an automobile accident as a young girl: "When I was sent to Rome as ambas-sador from the United States, I was a new Catholic — a convert. At my first audience with the Pope, he made me a wonderful gift. He gave me a small gold medallion inside of which is a sliver believed to be from the true cross. I am going to give it to you for this Chapel."

At the right of the altar is a gold baptismal font set with sapphires (see page 42). Behind it stands a stained-glass screen, a fragment from Lambeth Palace, the residence of the Archbishops of Canterbury, that a friend of Moore's picked up off the ground after a bomb-ing raid in World War II. She asked Moore to find a place for it in the castle.

BIBLE ON PRIE-DIEU
4" x 2¼" x ¾"

RUSSIAN ICON
1⅝" x 1⅜"

MONSTRANCE
4" x 1½" x 1½"

VIAL WITH CRUCIFIX
5⅛" x 1"

PAPAL SEAL
6¼" x 1½"

PAPAL SEAL DETAIL
6¼" x 1½"

THE GREAT HALL

3'-6" x 4'-3"

The formal entrance to the Fairy Castle,

the Great Hall, is the largest room in the house and serves as the picture gallery and museum. The architecture is appropriately grand, with a vaulted Gothic ceiling and a dramatic floating staircase that winds to the upper regions. The arched doorway features a carved overdoor frieze and is flanked by pillars. The etched ivory floor is painted a high-gloss finish and polished. Fixed floor-to-ceiling etched glass windows define one side of the room. THE DECOR OF THE GREAT HALL displays the same combination of fantasy and real-life treasures that marks the Fairy Castle as a whole. Evidence of the fairy-tale theme appears in the ceiling, painted with characters from the tales of the Brothers Grimm, and over the doorway, with a picture of the Pied Piper of Hamelin. Stories of Jack and the Beanstalk, the Princess and the Seven Swans, Prince Charming, and the Princess and the Doe are etched in the glass windows.

On the walls immortal comic-strip characters from the early 1900s share the limelight
with their more venerable fantasy counterparts: Walt Disney painted Mickey and
Minnie Mouse in the roles of the King and
Queen of Hearts. George MacManus, the
creator of "Jiggs and Maggie," painted
Jiggs as Old King Cole. Percy Crosby drew
his famous urchin, Skippy.

Fairy-tale objects are also proudly displayed as treasures. The chairs of the Three
Bears, carved from balsa wood, are
so small that each sits on the
head of an ordinary pin; the
largest weighs 150,000th of
an ounce. The chairs have
been placed under a glass
bell to protect them lest a
breath or sneeze blow them
away. Also prominently posi-
tioned on a table in the hall is the
Goose That Lays the Golden Eggs — along
with a basket of eggs already laid.

Cinderella's glass slippers likewise take
pride of place. Hollow, with high heels and
red bows, they are one-quarter-inch long.
Moore searched fruitlessly for such slippers
for years in Venice and Murano, and in Bo-
hemia and Scandinavia—wherever glass was
made. She obtained them at last unexpect-
edly, in the United States. She had described her unsuccessful search in an inter-

view to a reporter in Michigan. Shortly
thereafter, Moore received a letter from a
retired exhibition glassblower who had been
with the Ringling Brothers circus. He
thought he not only had the only pipe that
could blow anything so difficult, he had the
skill. He blew possibly the smallest glass
slippers ever conceived and made a present
of them to Moore.

The paintings that hang in the hall
are a combination of miniature copies
and original works of art. The tiny
portrait is a replica of the painting Leon Gordon made of
Moore in the gown she
wore in the film *Irene*. And
perhaps no object in the
Great Hall so exemplifies
the mixture of real life and
fantasy as the dollar-size miniature of Red Riding Hood, painted on ivory by Lisbeth Stone Barrett, a
well-known miniaturist.

In addition to all the minute copies
and fantasy creations in the Great Hall are
some genuine antiquities — tiny but au-
thentic museum treasures. The Great Hall
also is home every winter to the Fairy
Castle's Christmas tree. The very special
ten-inch tree, commissioned by Moore
to be handmade for the castle, is trimmed
with tinsel and precious stones.

MONG THE TREASURES OF THE Fairy Castle are three Egyptian statues less than an inch high that Moore believed to be over 2,000 years old (above left). The lapis-lazuli version (on the gold pedestal) was brought to Moore by an archaeologist friend from a dig in Egypt. The busts (above right) include a Roman bronze head from about the first century AD. The terra cotta Indian Madonna, from about 700 AD, comes from Delhi, and the terra cotta head is Greek, made about 2,000 years ago. Antique vessels (left) include a blue Syrian vase from 740 AD, presented to Moore by the curator of The Toledo Museum of Art in Ohio. The tiny Chinese jar given to Moore by the Museum of Art in Bangkok is about 1,000 years old.

BATTERSEA ENAMEL TABLE
2 ¼" x 3" x 2 ¼"

BUDDHA
5 ½" x 3 ¾" x 3"

CHEST
5 ¾" x 4 ¼" x 2 ¾"

DIAMOND IN GOLD CASKET
1 ¾" x ⅞" x 1 ⅛"

"CINDERELLA'S SLIPPERS"
1 ¼" x 1 ¼" x 1"

"THE KING AND QUEEN OF HEARTS"
WALT DISNEY
3 ⅝" x 4 ⅝"

JIGS AS OLD KING COLE
GEORGE MACMANUS
4 ½" x 3 ½"

"NARWHAL TUSK"
3" x ½" x ½"

GREEK HEAD
5 ½" x 2"

BATTERSEA ENAMEL LOVESEAT
3 ½" x 3 ⅛" x 1 ½"

BATTERSEA ENAMEL CHAIR
3 ⅛" x 2" x 2"

IVORY FIGURINE
6" x 1 ¼" x 1 ¼"

IN ADDITION TO THE TREASURES of the imagination are those that are copied from genuine historical masterpieces from all periods. Most prominent is the eighteenth-century French copy in ivory of Gianlorenzo Bernini's famous sculpture *The Abduction of Proserpina* (1621-22). The Battersea table used to display the wonderful Goose is complemented by the Battersea love-seat and chairs. The two silver-and-gold armored knights who guard the entrance to the Great Hall come from the collection of the great romantic film star of the 1920s Rudolph Valentino. The Crown Jewels, commissioned by a friend of Moore's and produced by Brock and Company, Los Angeles jewelers, are also kept in the Great Hall. The crown, trimmed with oriental pearls and a diamond-imbedded platinum star, has a shamrock-cut emerald beneath and rests in a gold box, engraved in Gaelic with the inscription: "Love never dies." The scepter, finished with a diamond-studded tip and a gold orb, completes the panoply. And finally, also in the realm of miniaturized versions of real-life objects, is an early American musket and small arms that are capable of firing. Rice-grain bullets for the musket and pistol have to be made in the little tool that resembles a nutcracker.

The castle is exactly like the dream of my childhood, except

that it is real. — COLLEEN MOORE

THE DRAWING ROOM

2'-3" x 3'-3"

Over the doorway that leads to the Drawing Room is a shield bearing the date of the first casting made for the Fairy Castle: 1928. The Drawing Room contains some of the castle's most precious and valuable decorations. The most distinguishing feature in the vaulted room is the perfectly scaled, exquisite chandelier, made from Moore's own diamond and emerald jewelry. The rose-quartz floor bordered in green jade, which was made in China, establishes the color scheme. George Townsend Cole, a Los Angeles artist who was intrigued by the castle and often came to watch during construction, contributed the mural depicting Cinderella. THE FURNISHINGS ARE RARE and elegant. The amber vases flanking the staircase are more than 500 years old and came from the collection of the last dowager empress of China. The suite of furniture is sterling silver; a chess table, with its minuscule board and men all set out for a game, is carved out of ivory. On the mantel is a tiny gold clock set with diamonds and emeralds to match the chandelier. A portrait of Moore by her friend the American illustrator James Montgomery Flagg sits in a silver frame on the table.

MORE FAIRY TALES, FROM THE BROTHERS GRIMM and from Hans Christian Andersen, are carved into the pillars that flank the staircase leading to the Princess' Bedroom and on to the turret.

COLLEEN MOORE DRAWING
BY JAMES MONTGOMERY FLAGG
1 ⅞" x ¾"

WRITING DESK
4 ¼" x 2 ⅛" x 1 ¼"

PIANO STOOL
WITH MUSIC BOOKS
1 ¾" x 2" x 1 ¼"

GRANDFATHER CLOCK
6 ⅛" x 2 ½" x 1 ⅜"

JEWELED MANTEL CLOCK
⅞" x 1 ¼" x ¼"

VIOLIN
2 ½" x ¾" x ¼"

ARMCHAIR
3 ¾" x 2 ¼" x 2"

CHESS TABLE
1 ½" x 1 ⅞" x 1 ½"

PIANO
2 ¾" x 6 ¼" x 3"

We'll have to think of all the things real people
couldn't have. — COLLEEN MOORE

THE DINING ROOM

2'-3" x 3'

King Arthur and the Knights of the Round Table forms the theme for the

decor of the Dining Room. Because most historians believe that Camelot itself was a legend and that Arthur, Guinevere, and the knights were products of the imagination, celebrated in song by medieval minstrels, the approach to the subject could be legitimately fanciful. The room has a high ceiling and arched doorways surmounted by broken pediments and flanked with twisted columns. The bare floor is highly polished and the beamed ceiling is lighted from above. Two tall pilasters between the arches on the main wall are topped with Corinthian capitals. THE CUPBOARD TO THE RIGHT displays more tiny treasures: a complete breakfast set of Royal Cauldon porcelain, painted in the Greek key pattern. The motif on the egg cups is so minute that it had to be painted with a single-haired brush. The collection of gold teapots once hung from one of Moore's charm bracelets. The decanter standing on the mahogany wine holder is Waterford made in Ireland well over a century ago. Additional miniature tableware and dining paraphernalia of all kinds fill the cupboards and serving pieces.

T HE SEMICIRCULAR DINING TABLE has chairs for the king and queen and the twelve knights; identifying coats of arms are painted on the back of each chair. Because Moore and her coconspirators had the freedom to invent the heraldic devices, they were able to refer to the love affair between Arthur's wife, Guinevere, and his best friend, Lancelot. Lancelot's shield bears a double cross and a snake in the grass; Guinevere's crest has two hearts entwined; and Arthur's device, which features his sword, Excalibur, also includes a broken heart.

The table service is gold; the plates were a gift from Moore's parents, and the cutlery came from her brother. The half-inch-long knives are marked with Moore's monogram. The gold goblets came from Mexico and the Bristol wine glasses are over a hundred years old.

Above the room's arches five needlepoint "tapestries" depict the Knights of the Round Table. These hangings were commissioned for the castle from Madame Jorey, a master needleworker who had an atelier in Vienna before World War II. It is almost impossible to distinguish the stitches in this true "petit point" without the aid of a magnifying glass. Only two women in the shop were capable of such fine work, which took many months to complete. The tapestries were finally hung in 1935.

CELLARET WITH
WATERFORD DECANTER
2 ¼" x 1 ¼", 1 ¼" x ⅝"

TAPESTRY
8" x 7"

DINING ROOM CHAIR
5 ⅜" x 3" x 2"

*…diminutive objects have come down to us from the dawn
of history.* — COLLEEN MOORE

THE KITCHEN

2'-3" x 1'-9"

Murals in the Kitchen celebrate

nursery rhymes and stories: Jack and Jill, Little Jack Horner, Humpty-Dumpty, Puss in Boots, the Lazy Grasshopper, and the Three Little Pigs. The legs of the kitchen table are carved to represent the King and Queen of Hearts. The Three Blind Mice on the stools are ivory. The tiny copper stove recalls the one in which the Wicked Witch locked Hansel and Gretel. The Royal Doulton dinner service displayed on the table is an exact replica of the one made for the fabled doll house in Windsor Castle made for Queen Mary; her crest appears on the rim of the tiny plates. The sole surviving memento of Moore's first doll house, the purple wine glass on the table, was originally from a set of six that decorated the cigar-box dining room of the house her father and mother built for her when she was a child.

COPPER COFFEEPOT
1 ½" x ⅞"

POT RACK
6 ½" x 6 ¼" x 2 "

COOKBOOK
1 ⅝" x 1" x ⅝"

A STORAGE ROOM ABOVE THE KITCHEN (FACING PAGE) houses extra china, glassware, and silver: the castle is equipped to serve large parties. The storeroom walls are decorated with appropriate murals: Mistress Mary Quite Contrary oversees the garden area; the Wicked Witch patrols the silver chests on her broomstick.

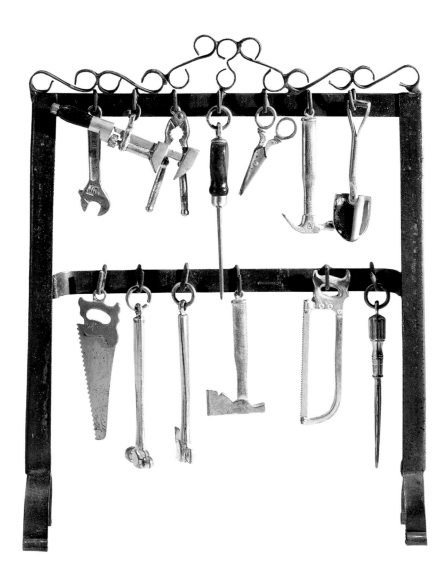

The child yearns to interpret the adult world in terms he can handle, and small replicas of
grown-up things answer his need. — COLLEEN MOORE

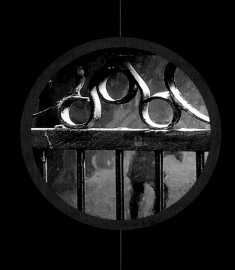

ALI BABA'S CAVE

8" x 1'-6"

THE REPLICA OF THE CAVE OF ALI BABA AND HIS Forty Thieves is filled with chests full of jewels that unlike the other gems in the castle, are gen-uinely make-believe. Colleen Moore sometimes mused that it might be wise to remove the chests to the Attic and instead install a sauna in the cave.

THE PRINCE'S BEDROOM

2'-3" x 2'

A bedroom is very personal—much more difficult to design without knowing the distinctive character of the individual in question.

For no known reason, Moore imagined an Eastern ancestry for the Prince, envisioning him as the descendent of a sultan or a czar, or perhaps a figure from a Persian fairy tale. THIS PRINCE'S BEDROOM was cast in bronze instead of the aluminum used for the rest of the castle, because Moore intended to send it to a colony of icon makers on the Volga River to have it decorated in baked enamel. This plan was never realized, so instead the theme of Little Czar Saltar was confined to carvings on the bed and chairs, and the walls were painted in Russian blue. THE FRESCOED CEILING is shaped like a canopy, supported by four ornate pillars. The three Japanese chests are made of gold inlaid with silver and iron: the smallest is over 500 years old; the middle-sized one is a century and a half old; and the largest one was commissioned in Kyoto in 1935. This last chest bears scenes from Moore's favorite Japanese fairy tales, accomplished by members of a family of craftsmen who have practiced their art for generations. IN THE CZAR SALTAR fairy tale is a wicked white bear, which inspired Moore to have a polar bear rug for the room. A taxidermist used the ermine skin Moore brought, then created the "bear's" ferocious teeth from those of a mouse. Near the bed are the sword Excalibur and a pair of gold running shoes.

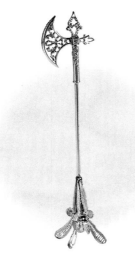

SILVER HALBERD
5 ¼" x 1 ¼"

LACQUER CHEST
1 ⅛" x 3 ⅝" x 2 ½"

JEWELED SWORD
3 ⅝" x 1"

GOLD RUNNING SHOES
¼" x 1" [EACH]

ENAMEL CHEST
2" x 2 ¾" x 1 ⅝"

ENAMEL BOOT
1 ½" x 1 ½" x ¼"

…numerous people… have offered their tiny treasures or their unusual skills
as gifts to the castle. — COLLEEN MOORE

MINIATURE OF THE
VIRGIN OF GUADALUPE
2½" x 1⅜"

ARMOIRE
7" x 3⅝" x 1"

FIREPLACE TOOLS
3" x 1½"

OVER THE PRIE-DIEU HANGS A REMARKABLE miniature on copper of the Virgin of Guadalupe (above left), painted by the well-known Mexican artist Ramos Martinez. Martinez made a pilgrimage to the Shrine of Guadalupe on behalf of his polio-stricken daughter, vowing to honor the Virgin at every opportunity if his daughter recovered. The child regained her health. When Martinez heard about Moore's nationwide tour to benefit children's hospitals, he asked to paint a portrait of the Virgin for the castle. This miniature was the exquisite result.

THE PRINCESS' BEDROOM

2'-3" x 3'

When Moore and her father were pondering over the floor of the Bedroom of the Princess, she thought of Sleeping Beauty's tiny bare feet running from her golden bed to her ivory dressing table. What material would be elegant enough? Gold was too hard, silver too cold, wood too common. The answer was mother-of-pearl, and Moore was convinced that Sleeping Beauty loved it. The mother-of-pearl mosaic has a gold-inlaid border. THE VERY SPACIOUS BEDROOM is almost two feet long and one-and-a-half feet wide. Since miniature-room height must be overscaled to produce the illusion of reality, the ceiling that looks about fourteen inches high is in reality twenty-four inches. The walls are painted pale pink with a mural of Peter Pan over the door leading to the Bathroom of the Princess. Delicate fairy-tale motifs decorate the domed ceiling and walls and outline the windows and the canopy of the bed. Stained-glass windows in the Gothic tradition decorate the back wall, with two chandeliers adding their light.

The Princess' boat-shaped bed with a diadem canopy is made of gold and dressed with a bedspread of golden spider web that covered her during her hundred-year wait for Prince Charming. The Battersea enamel chairs, brought from Paris by Moore's aunts when she was a child, are part of a set scattered throughout the castle, all bearing the same design engraved on the back.

A rarity here is the collection of miniature Bristol glass displayed on the three-tiered Battersea shelves. Most of this collection was given to Moore by complete strangers. She found them to be generous, always looking for a good home for an unneeded piece. The lady from Philadelphia who donated the purple cream jug and sugar bowl was insulted when Moore offered to pay for them: "I have been looking for a home for them for years. Please take them and treasure them and I will be able to die happy." The perfectly paired wee Staffordshire lambs were acquired in a similar fashion — from a previously unknown Boston collector who insisted: "But they belong here." The bird in the gilded cage is the Blue Bird of Happiness. It was presented to Moore by the Blue Bird Society of Dallas, and she considered it a good-luck piece. The red satin slippers resting on a hooked rug beside the Princess' bed are one-quarter-inch long and have hand-sewn leather soles. They were made by an Italian shoemaker who saw the castle on tour at R. H. Macy's in New York and became concerned for the Princess' bare feet. He determined to contrive for her the smallest pair of shoes in the world.

When Will Rousseau was photographing the rooms for Moore, she suggested that they ought to incorporate their own presence as a "signature." Rousseau made two photographic portraits: Moore's photograph stands on the silver table in the Drawing Room, Rousseau's in a frame on the Princess' dressing table.

*The Fairy Princess became so real to us [my father and me] that we
would speak of her in the most intimate terms. We felt we actually could see her,
although we each saw her differently.* — COLLEEN MOORE

THE PLATINUM CHAIRS SET WITH DIA–
monds were made by a jeweler in Des
Moines, Iowa, where the house was ex–
hibited on tour. The seats are green
cloisonné and the backs are made
from a pair of emerald and diamond
clips that Moore preferred to see in
the castle rather than on her lapel.

STAFFORDSHIRE LAMBS
⅞" x ¾" [EACH]

SPINNING WHEEL
4½" x 2" x 2"

UPRIGHT PIANO
3¾" x 1½" x 2½"

URN
3¼" x 1½"

SHELF WITH BRISTOL CHINA
3½" x 2¾" x 1¼"

STANDING CLOCK
5¼" x 2" x 1⅛"

THE GOLD-AND-DIAMOND TOILET SET on the carved ivory chest was made by Guglielmo Cini, a prominent Boston jewelry designer. The mirror and brush have a small platinum crown on their backs, and the platinum handles are encrusted with diamonds. To obtain hairs fine enough for the scale of the brush, Cini clipped the white guard hairs at the edge of his wife's silver-fox scarf. The complete set includes the brush and mirror, a tiny comb and nail file, and a powder box and jewel box, each no bigger than the nail of a little finger.

THE ROYAL BATHROOMS

PRINCESS' BATHROOM

2' x 1'-9"

PRINCE'S BATHROOM

1'-9" x 1'

Colleen Moore's own yellow onyx bath-

room was the height of luxury. She could do no less for the royal couple. The sea nymph Undine, whose story is etched on the back wall, provides the theme for the crystal-and-silver Bathroom of the Princess. The outstanding feature here is that water runs from the silver spigots in a stream as fine as a thread. The jars and bottles on the steps leading to the tub are filled with precious oils and perfumes. TRANSLUCENT ALABASTER FORMS the walls and tub of the Bathroom of the Prince. The tub itself is conceived as a highly stylized Chinese lily. Small turquoise Chinese guardian figures and decorative frogs adorn the tub; the mermaids are of gold. The dolphin-fauceted gold wash basin, in the form of a shell, rests on the tails of dolphins. Centered in the gold mirror above the basin is a lovely sapphire surrounded by diamonds, which came from a ring given to Moore by her grandmother.

LEFT: Princess' Bathroom

"I want the water to run and the lights to burn," he [my father] stated. "I have to think of function!" — COLLEEN MOORE

LEFT: Detail of faucet, Princess' Bathroom

ABOVE: Prince's Bathroom

On top of a gold chest inlaid with iron and silver is the Prince's
razor, complete with a removable steel blade.

THE ATTIC

2'-3" x 3'

EVERY HOUSE REQUIRES A STORAGE AREA FOR treasures, and the Fairy Castle is no exception. The Attic was designed and produced by Endre Vitez, a former art director of the Museum of Science and Industry, who for many years gave the castle his special attention. Something needed to be done to accommodate extra pieces, as Moore continued to donate artifacts to the museum. To avoid clutter, the Attic became the solution: shelves provide space for dishes and vases. Extra chairs, a silver sofa, and several Battersea stools are brought down only for special occasions. A silver samisen is stored here because no logical place in the main rooms could be found for it. Rumpelstiltskin's spinning wheel is suspended from the ceiling.

COLLEEN

MOORE

REEL

LIFE

Colleen Moore and her parents, Agnes Kelly Morrison
and Charles Morrison, c. 1925

In the early 1920s, a time when a prosper-ous nation wanted to have fun and Victorian ideals of maidenhood were beginning to feel unbearably restrictive to modern women, a best-selling book by Warner Fabian called *Flaming Youth* became a smash movie across America. Suddenly every young woman wanted to bob her hair, wear short dresses and unfastened galoshes — to be just like the original flapper, the girlish star of the 1923 film and the highest-paid actress in Hollywood: Colleen Moore. THE TALENTED AND THOUGHTFUL Colleen Moore was once one of the greatest and most beloved in Hollywood's con-stellation of silent stars. Born Kathleen Morrison in 1902, Moore described her childhood as idyllic, one in which she and her brother were the center of a close and loving family. From the age of five when she saw her first play, a production of *Peter Pan*, Moore knew she wanted to be an actress. And al-though the Morrisons were just a typical middle-class family, Moore's Aunt Libby was married to Walter Howey, editor of the *Chicago Examiner*, one of the city's major daily newspapers.

The childless Howeys doted on their niece and helped her break into the movie industry.

Walter Howey was a friend of film's first directorial giant, D. W. Griffith, who created the astonishing epics *Birth of a Nation* and *Intolerance*, both still noteworthy for their brilliance as well as their racism. Getting censors to approve such films was problematic, but Howey was able to be of assistance. When Griffith gratefully asked how he could repay the favor, Libby Howey replied: "We have a niece...." Shortly afterward, a long-distance phone call to the Morrison household in Tampa, Florida conveyed the unbelievable news that the world-famous D. W. Griffith was offering the fifteen-year-old Kathleen Morrison a six-month contract.

In 1916 Hollywood was still a small village, albeit growing wildly with the new medium of motion pictures that had begun only twenty years earlier. The freshly christened Colleen Moore (a name Walter Howey chose because he felt "Colleen" would appeal to Irish audiences and "Moore" would fit better on a marquee) traveled to Hollywood with her grandmother as chaperon. She accompanied Moore to the set each day, sitting off to the side knitting — and overseeing Moore's contracts. It was her grandmother who always told Moore to ask for more money after each picture — and who never thought she had asked for enough. Later, at the peak of her career when Moore told her grandmother that she had finally been given a contract for the incredible sum of $10,000 per week, she was scarcely surprised at the response: "You should have asked for $20,000."

While Moore's early films — she made nineteen of them between the ages of seventeen and twenty-one — were popular, and she played opposite some of Hollywood's most charismatic male stars, such as John Gilbert and John Barry-more, Moore felt that she was not going anywhere: she could not seem to make the leap from "featured player" to "star."

Moore's new husband, John Mc-Cormick, a press agent for her studio, First National, helped Moore to take the next step. McCormick wooed Moore assiduously — and promoted her pictures — building his own career in the process. Shortly after he and Moore became engaged, he became assistant to the head of production at First National. At the same time Moore determined to take a huge risk in order to distinguish herself from the other young movie actresses and get the part she wanted: the starring role in *Flaming Youth*. In order to persuade First National Studios to make her the star, she needed to change her image.

Years earlier Moore had realized that she had a knack for comedy, which she developed by studying with the comic geniuses of the time, such as director Mack Sennett, who had trained Charlie Chaplin, and with Chaplin himself. She also had realized that her looks were not those of conventional movie beauties. All the virginal roles Moore had played up to this point required long, beautifully curled hair, even if the style demanded hours of effort, as it did for Moore. Now she intended to make her unconventional looks and comedic training work for her: she cut her hair short.

The daring new look, combined with the acting skills she had polished over six years of hard work, won Moore the role of the heroine in *Flaming Youth*. The film became a national phenomenon, playing to packed houses everywhere, thrilling young people and shocking their parents. It featured Moore as a newly free-spirited, uninhibited character doing exactly as she pleased, even wearing unbuckled galoshes so that they flapped — just because it was fun and different.

STUDIO PUBLICITY
STILL

FROM THE
FILM "SO BIG"
1924

STUDIO PUBLICITY
STILL

MOORE'S EARLY FILMS WERE TYPICAL OF THE TIME, usually about sweet heroines being rescued from sneering villains by dashing young men. Moore and other young actresses — even the "older" women, such as Lillian Gish, Mary Pickford, and Gloria Swanson, who were then in their early twenties — often played children or adolescents in simple stories with happy endings. Female appearance was still governed by Victorian tradition: all young girls and unmarried women had long hair, worn down; married women and matrons still had long hair, worn up.

The portrayal of a liberated woman was so scandalous for the times that *Flaming Youth* was banned in Boston. And because so many college women emulated Moore's character by bobbing their hair and wearing flapping galoshes, a new word, "flapper," entered the nation's vocabulary.

The new look and the new attitude defined the 1920s. "I was the spark that lit up *Flaming Youth*," said F. Scott Fitzgerald, whose book *This Side of Paradise* also had helped to launch the new attitude of American youth. "Colleen Moore," he concluded, "was the torch."

Immediately a major Hollywood star, Moore redefined female attractiveness in a way that allowed any girl to be a flapper, not just those who met a particular standard of beauty. On her European honeymoon, she and her new husband, John McCormick, were

mobbed everywhere they went. Upon their return, Moore signed a new contract with First National that paid her the then-phenomenal sum of $4,000 a week; her husband was made head of production for the studio. They were the perfect Hollywood couple: young, rich, talented, and glamorous.

But despite the public image, the marriage was desperately unhappy from the outset. McCormick was an alcoholic who went on binges every six to eight weeks, starting with their wedding night. Moore tried to be understanding and forgave each episode. Nevertheless, as McCormick's career flourished along with hers and the studio's pressure on him mounted, so did his drinking.

As a distraction, Moore threw herself into making pictures and building a spectacular mansion in Hollywood. Harold Grieve, a studio art director, took over the house's interior design, creating one of the glorious Hollywood estates that hosted legendary parties. Moore spent over a quarter of a million dollars on the estate, then an exorbitant sum of money.

While Moore went on to one starring role after another, McCormick's drinking dramatically worsened. His work suffered and rumors of his drinking spread throughout Hollywood. The marriage was in serious trouble, but the devoutly Catholic Moore struggled with the idea of divorce. After a legal sep-

aration, Moore began seeing another man. On a binge, a devastated McCormick attempted suicide by swimming out to sea, but was rescued by friends. The poignant situation of a wife's soaring career and a husband's failure in Hollywood attracted attention, and McCormick's suicide attempt became

incorporated into the original screenplay for the film *A Star Is Born* (1935 and remade twice since), which was based loosely on the marriage of Moore and McCormick.

Moore's parents had moved to Hollywood to be near their daughter. Charles Morrison, to distract Moore from her troubles, suggested she resume a favorite interest from her childhood: realizing her doll-house dreams on a scale never seen before. Throughout her childhood, Moore had had a series of elaborate doll houses, each grander than the preceding one. The Fairy Castle would be the culmination of these childhood fantasies. Horace Jackson, Moore's set designer at First National, helped create the plans; Harold Grieve, who had designed Moore's own palatial home, was brought back to design the castle's spectacular interiors.

Colleen Moore and Edmund Lowe in
Happiness Ahead. c. 1925

126-18

STUDIO PUBLICITY
STILL

STUDIO PUBLICITY
STILL

STUDIO PUBLICITY
STILL

STUDIO PUBLICITY
STILL

FROM THE
FILM "WE MODERNS"
1924

STUDIO PUBLICITY
STILL

"I was the spark that lit up Flaming Youth," said F. Scott Fitzgerald, whose
book *This Side of Paradise* also had helped to launch the new attitude of American youth.
"Colleen Moore," he concluded, *"was the torch."*

The Fairy Castle became Moore's obsession: she enlisted the help of everyone she knew and spent nearly half a million dollars — an astounding amount of money in the 1920s and twice what she had spent on her fabulous Hollywood estate.

Moore made additional, more important, changes in her life. She divorced John McCormick, briefly married and then divorced a New York stockbroker, and finally decided to leave Hollywood altogether.

It had been a turbulent time for many in Hollywood. The new talkies took the industry by storm after Al Jolson starred in the first one, *The Jazz Singer*, in 1927. Some silent-movie stars made the transition, others failed. Famous silent-screen beauty Norma Talmadge destroyed her sultry, exotic image when her first speaking roles revealed her thick Brooklyn accent. The high-pitched voice of American heart-throb John Gilbert, the love of Greta Garbo's life, clashed with his silent-movie image. Careers disappeared almost overnight.

Moore, however, had little difficulty, and she continued to make popular comedies. What was not easy for her was growing up. In all her roles she had played young women, especially after she created the flapper craze. In her thirties, she sought out mature, dramatic roles, but her public disapproved. When she made what she considered her best film, *The Power and the Glory* in 1935 with Spencer Tracy, playing a character who ages more than thirty years, her previously loyal audiences stayed away. America wanted Moore to go back to playing young girls; she wanted to look only forward.

Moore needed to create a new role for herself. With Americans in the throes of the Great Depression, she decided that she could be of help, especially to children. In 1935 she took her Fairy Castle on a national tour to raise money for children's charities. The $650,000 she generated was an impressive amount of money in the depressed years of the 1930s.

While putting her fantasy creation to good use, Moore decided as well that having abandoned in her own life the glamour of Hollywood, she was ready to have for herself the private, "real life" enjoyed by more ordinary people. In Chicago she met Homer Hargrave, a widower with two young children who was one of the founders of Merrill Lynch. They married and Moore raised the children as her own. She rented her Hollywood mansion to a series of glamorous tenants, from Marlene Dietrich to Errol Flynn, and remained in Chicago, devoting her time to her family and doing extensive philanthropic work.

Following Homer Hargrave's death in 1964, Moore reinvented herself once again. She wrote her autobiography, then a book about the Fairy Castle, and finally a book about investing, *How Women Can Make Money in the Stock Market*, based on the enormous wealth she had created through shrewd investments. She also helped found the Chicago International Film Festival.

Occasionally visiting Hollywood to check on her mansion, which she maintained as an investment, Moore once welcomed her old friend Greta Garbo to the house that had been the site of countless parties during Hollywood's glory days. Garbo looked around the spectacular estate, then turned to Moore and said, "Ah, Colleen, those were the good old days." That may have been true for Garbo, but not for Colleen Moore. When she died at age eighty-five in 1988, she left a legacy that included over sixty films and her favorite passion, the Fairy Castle, which continues to draw millions of visitors to Chicago's Museum of Science and Industry.

MOORE'S CHILDHOOD DREAM REMAINS ALIVE today, and no one put it better than Moore herself: *"A dream is a gift given us at birth by our Fairy Godmother… a lovely gossamer thought that floats in the secret part of our imaginations most of our lives. I was one of the lucky ones, for my dream came true."*

TRANSCRIPTS OF

BOOKS

IN THE CASTLE

LIBRARY

SELECTED TRANSCRIPTIONS ARE
REPRODUCED EXACTLY
AS WRITTEN. NO CORRECTIONS
HAVE BEEN MADE.

EDWARD ALBEE
A Delicate Balance, 1966 *(play)*

"Time happens to people.
Everything becomes....too late,
finally. You know its going on....
up on the hill; you can see the dust,
and hear the cries,
and the steel....
but you wait....
and time happens
when you do go.... sword,
shield.... finally....
there's nothing there....
save rust; bones; and the wind."

Author's note: this speech
was written in August, 1966,
in Montauk Long Island,
while the body of the play
was composed in Europe
the spring of the same year.
These pages are gratefully
dedicated to Colleen Moore
and are written here on the first
of September, 1966 at Montauk
by Edward Albee, who is proud
to have this tiny book in such
large company.

HERVEY ALLEN
Anthony Adverse

Autographed for the dolls of Miss
Colleen Moore's doll house
by Hervey Allen

LOUIS BROMFIELD
A Good Woman

For Colleen Moore in Souvenir of
all the good times she has given
so many of us in the theatre and in
her own hospitable home. May she
have good luck and good friends
for ever and ever. With the affec-
tion and good wishes of Louis
Bromfield

BROWNE
This Believing World

Of all the autographs for which
I've ever been asked, this is far and
away the most delightful. I fear
for the spiritual health and moral
stability of your dolls after reading this wicked book. If it does
harm to grown Methodists, what will
it do to dolls?

With fervor,
Lewis Browne

(delivered by the hand of
Carmelita Geraghty.
May 30 XXVIII)

EDGAR RICE BURROUGHS
Tarzan: First Edition

Chapter I
The little Princess was walking
in the garden when a bad thought
sneaked up behind her and whispered in her ear, "Go into the forbidden forest." "Hi-Lee! Oh, no!
Oh, no! Yodeled

[FACING PAGE ILLUSTRATION:
MULTI-COLORED, BOY IN FOREST]

the little princess, "My mama said I
mustn't go into the forbidden forest, and my papa said she ought to

[ILLUSTRATION: MULTI-COLORED,
OF FEMALE IN GRASS SKIRT
WINKING]

know." "But, but" butted the bad
thought, "Everything that you
shouldn't do everything that you
mustn't do are in the forbidden
forest, and they

[ILLUSTRATION: MULTI-COLORED,
OF HALF-HUMAN HALF ANIMAL
WITH PITCHFORK]

include about everything it's fun
doing. Think what a good time you
could have."

So the little princess put a nutty
hamburger in a shoe box for her
lunch,

[ILLUSTRATION: MULTI-COLORED,
BOX NUMBERED IN SIZE 3 WITH
HAND PUTTING HAMBURGER IN BOX]

vaulted over the garden wall and
went into the forbidden forest.

[ILLUSTRATION; MULTI-COLORED,
SIGN THAT SAYS "*Forbidden forest
keep out*"]

Chapter 2
The little princess had not gone
far into the dark and gloomy wood
when she met Histah the snake.

[ILLUSTRATION; MULTI-COLORED,
SNAKE HANGING FROM TREE
WITH LITTLE GIRL LOOKING UP]

"Have an apple" Invited Histah.
"What for?" Asked the little
princess. "It will keep the doctor
away." Replied Histah, pulling
on his long black mustache. "But
if I eat

[ILLUSTRATION; MULTI-COLORED,
FACE OF SNAKE WITH WORD *Histah*]

it, I may need the doctor,"
Countered the little princess with
her left. "Ah, Ha! Foiled again,"
Hissed Histah. "Not so fast." Cried
the little princess.

[ILLUSTRATION: MULTI-COLORED,
SNAKE, GIRL AND HALF-
MAN/HALF-HUMAN WITH
PITCHFORK]

"Gimme the apple," For the bad
thought had again whispered in her
ear.

[ILLUSTRATION: MULTI-COLORED APPLE]

Chapter 3
The little princess was about to eat the apple when Tantor the elephant

[ILLUSTRATION; MULTI-COLORED, ELEPHANT WITH GIRL]

barged up and took it way from her, "Beat it!" He trumpeted at Histah: Then he ate the apple himself. "What have you in that shoe box?" He asked.

[ILLUSTRATION: MULTI-COLORED, ELEPHANT IN THE FOREST]

"A nutty hamburger," Replied the little princess. "Mercy me!" Swore Tantor. "What's the matter with it? — Dementia Praecox?" "No, just plain

[ILLUSTRATION: BLACK AND WHITE, ELEPHANT'S HEAD ENTITLED *Tantor Coming*]

nutty" Replied the little princess. "Well, you never can tell when it might develop a homicidal mania," Said Tantor. "Give it to me." So he took the nutty hamburger

[ILLUSTRATION: MULTI-COLORED, SIGN POINTING *next page*]

and ate that too: Then he, went away from there into the land of ptomaine.

[ILLUSTRATION: BLACK AND WHITE, ELEPHANTS HIND QUARTERS ENTITLED *Tantor going*]

Chapter 4
The little princess was very hungry; so she went deeper into the dark, damp wood looking

[ILLUSTRATION: BLACK AND WHITE, FOREST WITH LITTLE GIRL]

for another snake with an apple. But she didn't see Numa the lion stalking her. Numa, too, was very hungry; and as there are not many calories in stalks, he planned on

[ILLUSTRATION: MULTI-COLORED, LION]

eating the little princess. With a terrific roar, he leaped for her. The little princess turned, horror stricken; when to her amazement, she saw a

[ILLUSTRATION: MULTI-COLORED, VIEW OF THE PRINCESS]

bronzed giant, naked but for a G String, drop from an over-hanging branch full upon the tawny back of the carnivore. It was Tarzan Jr.!

[ILLUSTRATION: MULTI-COLORED, TARZAN JR. JUMPING FROM A TREE]

Once, twice, thrice his gleaming blade sank deep into the side of the great cat: and as Numa sank lifeless to the mottled sword, the lord of the

[ILLUSTRATION: MULTI-COLORED, BOY ATTACKING LION]

jungle placed a foot upon the carcass of his kill, raised his face to the heavens, and voiced the victory cry of the bull ape.

[ILLUSTRATION: MULTI-COLORED, TARZAN JR. STANDING ON BLEEDING LION WITH THE PRINCESS IN THE BACKGROUND]

Chapter 5
The little princess was still hungry. "Let's eat the lion," She said; "Unless you happen to

[ILLUSTRATION; PRINCESS AND TARZAN STANDING BACK TO BACK WITH BLOOD DRIPPING FROM HIS KNIFE]

have an apple in your pocket." "I haven't any pocket," Admitted Tarzan Jr. "All right then," Said the little princess, "Let's skip it."

[ILLUSTRATION; MULTI-COLORED, JUMP ROPE]

So Tarzan Jr. uncoiled his rope and they skipped, and skipped and skipped; and then they got married and lived happily for —

[ILLUSTRATION: MULTI-COLORED, TARZAN JR. AND THE PRINCESS SKIPPING ROPE]

ever after — and that is what the little princess got for disobeying her mama and going into the forbidden forest.

[ILLUSTRATION; MULTI-COLORED, SIGN THAT SAYS *"Forbidden forest keep out"* WITH RED X OVER THE SIGN]

JAMES M. CAIN
The
Postman
Always
Rings
Twice
By
James M. Cain

They
threw
me
off
the
hay
truck
around
noon.

WILLA CATHER
Shadow on the Rock

Quebec is to me the most interesting city in the world, but San
Francisco is
next.

AGATHA CHRISTIE
Bertram's Hotel

In the heart of the West End, there
are many evil pockets.

IRVIN S. COBB
Old Judge Priest

Judge Priest says "The laughter of
happy children must shorely be the
music of the spheres that the angels
in heaven dance to."

DAPHNE DU MAURIER
Rebecca

Last night I dreamed I went to
Manderly again. It seemed to me I
stood by the gate leading to the
drive, and for awhile I could not
enter for the way was barred to me.
There was a padlock and a chain
upon the gate. I called in my dream
to the lodge-keeper, and had no
answer, and peering over through
the rusty spokes of the gate I saw
that the lodge was uninhabited. No
smoke came from the chimney and
the little lattice windows gaped for-
lorn. Then, like all dreamers, I was
possessed of a sudden with super-
natural powers and passed like a
spirit through the barrier before me.
The drive wound away in front of
me, twisting and turning as if it
had always done, but as I advanced I
was aware that a change had come

upon it; it was narrow and unkept,
not the drive that we had known. At
first I was puzzled and did not
understand, and it was only when I
bent my head to avoid the low
swinging branch of a tree that I
realized what had happened.
Nature had come into her own again
and, little by little, in her stealthy,
insidious way had encroached upon
the drive with long, tenacious
fingers. The woods, always a men-
ace even in the past, had tri-
umphed in the end. They crowded,
dark and uncontrolled, to the bor-
ders of the drive. The beeches with
white, naked limbs leant close to
one another, their branches inter-
mingled in a strange embrace,
making a vault above my head like
the archway of a church. And there
were other trees as well, trees that
I did not recognize, squat oaks and
tortured elms that straggled cheek
by jowl with the beeches, and had
thrust themselves out of the quiet
earth along with monster shrubs
and plants, none of its former self,
with gravel surface gone, and
choked with grass and moss. The
trees had thrown out low branches,
making an impediment to progress;
the gnarled roots looked like
skeleton claws. Scattered here and
there amongst this jungle growth
I would recognize shrubs that had
been landmarks in our time, things
of culture and grace, hydrangeas
whose blue heads had been famous.
No hand had checked their progress,
and they had gone native now,
rearing to monster height without a
bloom, black and ugly as the name-
less parasites that grew besides
them. On and on, now east, now

west, wound the poor thread that
once had been our drive. Sometimes I thought it lost, but it
appeared again, beneath a fallen
tree perhaps, or struggling on
the other side of a muddied ditch
created by the winter rains. I had
not thought the way so long. Surely
the miles had multiplied, even as
the trees had done, and this path
led but to a labyrinth, some choked
wilderness, and not to the house
at all. I came upon it suddenly; the
approach masked by the unnatural
growth of a vast shrub that spread
in all directions, and I felt my
heart thumping in my breast, the
strange prick of tears behind my
eyes. There was Manderly, our
Manderly, secretive and silent as it
had always been, the grey stone
shining in the moonlight of my
dream, the melanoid windows
reflecting the green lawns and ter-
race. Time could not wreck the
perfect symmetry of those walls,
nor the site itself, a jewel in the
hollow of a hand.

LLOYD C. DOUGLAS
Magnificent Obsession, 1929

It has been said of this book that
the people who read it are never
quite the same again.

ALLEN DRURY
Advise and Consent

When Bob Munson awoke in his
apartment in the Sheraton Park
Hotel in Northwest Washington, he
knew it was going to be a bad day.

He went to the door to bring in the morning Washington Post he was convinced of it. PRESIDENT NAMES LEFFINGWELL TO BE SECRETARY OF STATE, the paper said. What Bob Munson said was, "Oh, God damn,"...

WARNER FABIAN
Flaming Youth

To Miss Moore who is the author's idea of "Flaming Youth."

EDNA FERBER
So Big

Inscribed for Colleen Moore
Sincerely —
Edna
Ferber

F. SCOTT FITZGERALD
This Side of Paradise

I was the spark that lit up
Flaming Youth
and Colleen Moore
was the torch.
What little things we are
to have caused all that
TROUBLE!

Chapter I
Amory Blaine inherited from his mother all the traits except a
stray
inexpressible
few
that
made
him
worth
while
?

GENE FOWLER
Father Goose

For Colleen Moore — niece of my great friend, Walter Howey
— Gene Fowler   Oct – 1934

[ON LAST PAGE, UPSIDE DOWN]

ELLEN GLASGOW
The Shadowy Third

The Shadowy Third and Other Stories by Ellen Glasgow made by L.H. Jenkins, Inc. Richmond, Virginia Presented to Miss Colleen Moore for her doll house Library by W.S. Rhodes
July 16, 1968

[BOOK IS A PRINTED COPY OF THE SHORT STORY "THE SHADOWY THIRD"]

H. W. GRIEVE
Interior Bold

California homes decorated by H. W. Grieve A.I.D.
Colleen Moore Boudoir, Bel-Air. Day bed upholstered in peach satin stripe taffeta

[PHOTO NEXT PAGE]

It is most important that the house should be
a perfect background for the occupant both in
color and type of decoration.

H. W. Grieve A.I.D.
1935

EDGAR A. GUEST
Home

It takes a heap o' livin'
2 in a house to make
3 it home

a heap o' sun an' shadder
an' ye sometimes have to roam
afore ye really 'preciate
the things ye left behind
An hunger fer 'em somehow,
with 'em always on your mind
It don't make any difference
how rich ye get te be
How much your chairs
an tables cost — How great
your luxury
It ain't home to ye
though it be
the Palace of a King
Until somehow your soul
is sort o' wrapped
Round Everything

For Miss Colleen Moore
Jan 30, 1936

WILLIAM RANDOLPH HEARST

My dear Miss Moore

I do not think that I can get all the nice things which I should like to say about you and your delightful doll house in this small book. But I can say that you are doing fine work, fine work with the little doll house, and you are giving joy to many children throughout the nation. You are benefiting many, many charities and you are allowing many people to see and to know better the lovely lady they have seen and admired on screen. Your friends feel that you are giving too much time to the dolls and to your charitable projects, and not enough time to them. That is a selfish view no doubt but a natural one. I deem it a great privilege to be invited to write in this volume and be in the doll house. I assume that when a man is very bad he sits in the dog house and when he is very good he gets in the doll house. I do not think that I deserve the distinction but I am very glad to be in such good company. May I make a suggestion with regard to the other occupants of the establishment. Why not dress up dolls in all the characters you have played on the screen and make background. Would not the public be delighted to see these characters live again, I know I would be. From my place in this little book on the shelf — and I am on the shelf in more ways than one. I could look down on the other occupants of the house and review many pleasant hours.

JAMES HILTON
Goodbye, Mr. Chips

When you are getting on in years (but not ill, of course) you get very sleepy at times, and the hours seem to pass like lazy cattle moving across a landscape.

RUPERT HUGHES
George Washington

George Washington could tell a lie
    — on
a good occasion. But I cannot tell
    a lie —
on this occasion. And so I say without
    out
fear of successful contradiction —
    that
Colleen Moore is an adorable
    actress
and an adorable child and I am
proud and glad to know her
and to sign my name as
her admirer and friend.

FANNIE HURST
Humoresque

F
A
N
N
I
E
H
U
R
S
T.

[ONE LETTER PER PAGE]

ALDOUS HUXLEY

How clear under the trees,
How bright the melody flows!
Running from one still pool to
    another
Into the lake of silence.

ROBINSON JEFFERS
The Low Sky

No vulture is here, hardly a hawk,
Could long wings or great eyes fly
Under this low-lidded sift sky?
On the wide heather the curlew's
    whistle
Dies of its echo, it has no room
Under the low lid of this tomb.
But one to whom mind and imagi-
    nation
Sometimes used to seem burden-
    some
Is glad to lie down awhile in the
    tomb.
Among stones and quietness
The mind dissolves without a
    sound,
The flesh drops into the ground.

SINCLAIR LEWIS
Arrowsmith

Chapter I
When Arrowsmith got sick
of discovering nasty bacilli,
he went to Hollywood,
hoping to get a job as an extra &
to see Colleen

Chapter II
He didn't

Chapter III
So he went back home

And in vast indignation
he bit a bacillus typhosus so
that it died of lock jaw.

Chapter IV
Dedicated to Colleen Moore.

ANITA LOOS
Gentlemen Prefer Blondes

A gentleman
friend and I
were dining
at the Ritz
last evening
and he said
that if
I took
a pencil
and a paper
and put down
all of my
 thoughts
it would
make
a book.

Anita Loos

CLARE BOOTH LUCE
The Woman

So I said to Howard, "What do you
    expect me to do?

Stay home and darn your socks?
  What do we all have money fo[r]?
Why do we keep servants?
— Silvia

opening lines of "The Woman"
Clare Booth Luce

FRANCES MARION
Valley People

Lovely April. I have come to
my little valley in the
foothills of Northern California.
As I climb to the top of a
rocky hill on my father's farm,
I can see the homes of my childhood
friends of twenty five years ago.
The pattern of the small farms
has not changed. Trees have grown
taller, that's all. The madione trees
are measuring their height
with the eucalypti, but
from my hill I can see
above their feathered crest.
Madione trees bring back
a rush of memories, their
bark is a tablet that
records the first secret
loves of youth.
The scent of new-mown
hay fills the air.
The pine-clad mountains
are purple silhouettes
against a sky amber with sunset.
Fluid geese on quiet wings
flying a high arc
toward the hidden
mountain lakes.
Peace lies in the valley in its gnarled
oaks, its full-breasted
catalpa trees, and the hushed
  mountains beyond.

To Colleen Moore a great artist
and loyal friend. Frances Marion

BRUCE MARSHALL
Bel-Air

"I sometimes think that
if it hadn't been for
the British soldier's
inveterate habit of
swilling his belly
with tea in
the middle of the
morning and the
afternoon the war would have been
won two years sooner."

CHARLES NORRIS
Bread

Frontispiece [CARTOON OF PERSON
READING BOOK ONLY SOLES OF
SHOES, HANDS AND TOP OF HEAD
VISIBLE]

For Colleen Moore —
From Chas. G. Norris

KATHLEEN NORRIS
For Colleen's Doll House

This little but very important book
  is written
by Colleen's friend Kathleen
  Norris, with love
for all the little living dolls who will
  some
day be the happier because God
  gave the world
a Colleen Moore.

MARY RENAULT

"Go to the Gods unconquered
  Alexander. May the River of
  Ordeal be mild as milk to you and
  bathe you in the light, not fire.
  May your dead forgive you; you

have given more life to me than you
brought death. God made the bull
to eat the grass, but the lion not;
and God alone will judge between
them. You were never without
love; where you go, may you find it
waiting."

From *The Persian Boy*

Spoken by Bogoas at Alexander's
death. M.R. December 22nd 1976

KENNETH ROBERTS
[BLANK COVER]

The Northwest Passage in the
  imagination
of all people, is a short cut to fame,
fortune and romance, a hidden
  route to
Golconda and the mystic East.

ADELA ROGERS ST. JOHNS
Sky Rocket

To Colleen Moore with all my love
and friendship —

GEORGE BERNARD SHAW
Saint Joan

Once there was a fairy prissess and
a fairy prince and They were having
fun in the palace and The prince
asked The prissess to dance and The
prissess sid yes so the both danced
and what do you Think happened
The prince steppd on the prissess's
lace gown and the Queen was very
Sad But The King said do not
worry. Queen But where will get
the money To Buy another one The
King said we'll have to earn it. But
how will we do said the Queen we
will [ho] to do hard work But what

is The hard work well heres some
work is sume house work and I will
do hard thinking But what will you
think well I will think important
said the King The Queen Said That
woodint make a enough maney O
yes it wod if we worken — of Said
the King The Queen Said you I
will do it So The next day the both
went To The To Sume house and
The Could get a job so The sun got
a nag maney So That The could
get a enoug—g maney To pay [for]
The lace gown and The prissess's
lace gown and The prissess was so
happy [an] that she hat o dance
and the King Said he would dance
with harsa The King was varry
careful To not step on The gown
and the prince was so happy That
The prissess had hah lace gown So
the King Said he wud lat The prince
dance with the prissess

The end

[TEXT WRITTEN BACK TO FRONT
WITH BOOK UPSIDE DOWN]

JOHN STEINBECK
Of Mice and Men

1. A few miles south of sale island,
the Salmon River drops in close to
the hillside bank and runs deep
and green. The water is warm, too
for it has slipped twinkling on the
yellow sand in the sunlight before
reaching the warmer pool.

John Steinbeck
Los Gatos 1936

DONALD OGDEN STEWART
Mr. & Mrs. Haddock Abroad

Dear Doll:
I hope that you have a very small
book worm to go with this.

Gratefully, Donald Ogden Stewart

IRVING STONE
The Agony and the Ecstasy

He sat before the mirror
of the second floor bedroom
sketching his lean cheeks

BOOTH TARKINGTON
Alice Adams
Tiffany Thayer

T
I
F
F
A
N
Y
T
H
A
Y
E
R

[ONE LETTER PER PAGE]

Put
them
all
together
they
spell
"mother"

A
word
that
means
the

world
to
me
!
F
I
N
I
S

Tiffany
Thayer

HENDRICK WILLEM VAN LOON
The Story of Mankind

[PRINTED IN INK WITH INK DECO-
RATIONS AROUND BORDERS]

[INK SKETCH OF MOUNTAIN, FOUR
LINES OF PRINTING TOO SMALL TO
BE READ]

[WATER COLORED SKETCH OF TWO
COLUMNS]

[WATER COLORED SKETCH OF AQUE-
DUCT] *Rome*

[WATER COLORED SKETCH OF CLIFF
WITH BOAT IN WATER AT BASE]

[WATER COLORED SKETCH OF
SAILING SHIP]

[WATER COLORED SKETCH OF
CASTLE ON HILL]

[WATER COLORED SKETCH OF SAIL-
ING SHIP]

[WATER COLORED SKETCH OF TWO
BLUE SHAPES, STACKED, RESEMBLES
ROCKET] *N*

[WATER COLORED SKETCH OF
BUILDING WITH ONION DOMES]

[WATER COLORED SKETCH OF
ELEPHANT WITH CARRIER ON BACK]

[WATER COLORED SKETCH OF
ELEPHANT WITH CARRIER ON BACK]

HUGH WALPOLE
Vanessa

At
the
sight
of
her
son
Judith's
eyes
and
mouth
broke
into
the
loveliest
smile
that
any
member
of
the
Hemies
family
had ever seen.

Hugh Walpole

WASHINGTON
His Farewell Address, 1932
Kingsport Press Inc.
Kingsport, Tenn.

Acknowledgment
The text of the address is taken,
with a few slight alterations, from
the volume *American Masterpieces*,
of the fifteen-volume set *Modern
Eloquence*.

[FOREWORD AND TEXT FOLLOW ON
148 PRINTED PAGES. TEXT PRINTED
IN FOUR IDENTICAL VOLUMES
EXCEPT THAT THREE HAVE BLUE
COVERS AND ONE IS BROWN.]

THORNTON WILDER
The Ides of March

Dear Colleen Moore,
It's been a pleasure to inscribe
this miniature book. May the Doll's
House continue its beneficent
journeys. With many regards and
much admiration devotedly.

Thornton Wilder

ALBERT RHYS WILLIAMS
Through the Russian Revolution

The cruiser AURORA firing over the
      winter
palace of the Tsar. Dull and
      muffled out of
the distance it comes, a requiem to
      king (?)
The death of the old order, a salu-
      tation to the new.
It is the voice of the masses thun-
      dering the demand
"All Power to the Soviets."

BEN A. WILLIAMS
House Divided

"As long as we
keep looking
back over our
shoulders, we'll
be forever
stumbling. When we
learn to
forget, then
we will go ahead."

THYRA S. WINSLOW
Picture Frames

Happiness
Ella was a rich girl. She had everything but she was not happy. One
day a poor little girl came to her
house. Ella gave the poor little girl

a doll and a doll buggy and her
biggest box of candy, and a dress
too, and other things to wear. And
then Ella was happy because she
had done things for others, because
she had given things to a little girl
who had none.

By Thrya Samter
7 years old

Footnote to Happiness
This, as nearly as I can rewrite it
is my first story, dictated to my
mother who sent it to a story con-
test where it got a prize of one
dollar. I never recovered. I am glad
to note that in spite of the simple
philosophy of life of my rather smug
first heroine she was not entirely
a fool — she did not give away her
doll house.

TWS

and
here
is
the
blot

[ARROW POINTS TO INK BLOT]

I
nearly
made
on
every
page.

The End